CONTE

LOOKING FOR LOVE

THROUGH THICKER LENSES

A Guide to Dating Later in Life

SHARON P. S. MARX

Dear Penny —
LIVE VIVIDLY !

Sharon PS Marx

ISBN 978-1-935497-98-1

Printed in the United States of America

Book design by Scott Stortz

Produced and distributed by

Butler Books
info@butlerbooks.com

"Do you have someone?"

"No. But I have a dream of someone."

— *You've Got Mail,* 1998 film

DATING COMES OF AGE

I don't pretend to be a psychologist, a therapist, or a counselor, although I am a certified teacher. What is relevant is that I am one of a growing group of aging hopefuls repeatedly cast into the dating marketplace for what, one fervently prays each time, will be *the last time*. And when it isn't, the incredulous reaction is always *"NOT AGAIN!"*

With this book, I hope to ease your reentry into the dating world. My primary purpose is to provide insight and optimism into what, as we age, often immobilizes us into missing if not the *best* time of our lives, then a very special alternative.

I have written this guide in an easy-to-follow and often lighthearted format. When we can smile at ourselves, we can accept who we are. And accepting who we are allows us to forgive our past as we embrace our present and our future.

Many years ago, Anthony Quinn, the title character in the film *Zorba the Greek*, exultantly proclaimed, "Each time is the first time!" He was referring to sexual encounters. But that's how I feel about dating experiences. Each time *feels* like the first time. And often, the first time isn't so good!

Yet, here we are, contemplating embarking upon *another* "first time."

As a young woman, I didn't like dating. And I don't like it now. I don't like waiting by the phone, but I don't like making cold calls, either. I don't like the preening part, and I don't like the screening part. I don't like getting to know someone. I want to meet a man and have already known him for 10 years. I want to feel as though he is as familiar as an old sweater with worn elbow patches.

It takes so long and so much effort to discover another person's essence. But I know that there's no way to circumvent the fact that *dating* is the only way to accomplish this.

I have been married more than once. And behind each failed marriage has been a woman confounded by either her inability to anticipate relationship problems or her disappointment at not being able to find mutually agreeable solutions when problems arise. I never anticipated divorce. I was going to be married for 57 or more years, like my parents and grandparents.

After the shock of each of my "untimely disconnects" passed, I wished that there had been actual rules for dating again, rules that every dating hopeful was required, nay, honor bound, to follow: rules that would help to assure us that the dating game would be played fairly and successfully.

I *wanted* to play, but obviously I had to be rewired. So I set out on a quest to change the fate my history seemed to be creating for me.

Then, an epiphany: the *process* of dating is pretty much the same now as it was 40 years ago. The problems occur because the *players* are different. At our more advanced ages, we don't have the energy we used to have. We also don't have as much time.

We are no less concerned about how we look than we ever were. But now there's less we can do about it.

Change happens! We must adjust our medicine regimen to our romantic dinner schedules. We bend to shave our legs and our backs go out. We can't paint our own toenails because we can't reach them. We're short of breath during sex. We spend eons in the bathroom, and if someone is waiting for us in the bedroom, we emerge making excuses and apologies. We sport tushies resembling elephant hide and breasts resembling dead fish. We suspect that dust bunnies are infiltrating our minds. We have polka-dotted hands and floppy earlobes and hair protruding from every orifice. We could have had roles in *Star Wars*. Our one consolation is that ultimately, we do see one another in softer focus—due to advancing cataracts.

These dilemmas are magnified by the self-inflicted humiliation or even shame we feel at our metamorphosis.

So what do we do when we sincerely wish to grow old in the company of a best friend and possible lover? First, we have to believe that we are dealing with the *opposite* sex and not the *opposing* one—no matter our sexual persuasion.

We will never be 100 percent certain of what we are doing, or whom we are doing it with. We *do* have to act on a bit of faith. Trust supposedly reigns victorious. But there are no guarantees, no verbal promises to which anyone can be held legally accountable.

I became determined to find some answers . . . some guidelines that would pave the way for those of us who, in our fifties and beyond, have found ourselves alone, cut off from long-term marriages or relationships, either by death or by design. Or who, after self-imposed, prolonged, celibate hiatuses, are ready to consider dating again.

My initial informational sources were my own memories and experience, which, while far more vast than I might have wished, never quite proved effective enough to assuage my own fears of growing older—by myself.

I read, I studied, I questioned others. I shared my concerns, thoughts, and ideas with them; and I discovered that I'm not the only fearful one. Many of us are anxious and stymied by our dating misconceptions and expectations. Everything about dating *again* feels new to us.

Dating is daunting at any age! Why, I asked myself, do we have to incorporate years of anxiety, insecurity, and skepticism into the mix?

This question plagued me as I continued to read, study, and interview other singles in their fifties, sixties, seventies, eighties, and beyond. Our problems appear widespread.

Thus, I have attempted to create a sort of template, a guide for those of us who find ourselves struggling with deciphering dating code demons. (Did we ever dream that we would be grandparents exploring dating on paths parallel to those of our grandchildren?)

The famed Cheshire Cat in *Alice in Wonderland* said, "If you don't know where you're going, any road will do."

Newsflash! *Any* road will *not* do.

You need a plan. You need a goal. You need resolve. You need optimism. You need direction. You need to open up to possibilities. You need to feel good about what you have chosen to do. You need to approve of *you*! And even if you are still uncomfortable, still afraid . . . if you want to reap the spoils, you have to enter the game.

So grab your glasses and let's explore the possibilities.

A ship in harbor is safe, but that is not what ships are built for.

— John Augustus Shedd

WHY?

A number of years ago, when I was dating a particular gentleman, we frequently ran into a mutual friend. Every time we met, our friend would look at me quizzically and simply ask, "Why?" Then all three of us would laugh. But years later, when I was single again, my friend reminded me of what he used to ask me. "I could never understand why you were with him," my friend explained. "Underneath my teasing, I was quite serious! You two just didn't seem to fit."

Later still, looking back on my relationship, I had to wonder: Did my wanting to be in a relationship so badly color my judgment? This question led me to focus on the reasons most people . . . *particularly* we who've reached the "Age of Reason". . . date.

Here are what I deem to be the *most common reasons* we are

"relationship seeking":

- We are longing for a significant human connection.
- We enjoy sex and want a sexual partner.
- We desire uncomplicated companionship.
- We are determined to alleviate boredom (which is often an issue after retirement).
- We are hoping to find or fit into a new social circle.
- We are hoping to expand our existing social circle.
- We just want to have fun.
- We need financial support or assistance.
- We are trying to prove to our ex that we are desirable.
- We are lonely and feeling a void.
- We are suffering from the empty bed syndrome.

While I hope, in my lists, to hit upon the *primary reasons* for begging the "to date or not to date" point, I may have missed yours! But you can fill in your own blanks. The point is that there is usually a reason why we are dissatisfied with our solitary state and *that one reason* is enough to spark our interest in dating again.

Some of us have *no* desire to date, and here is a partial list of the reasons why this is true:

- We don't want to make another mistake.

- We believe there can only be one true love in our lives.
- We think we look ugly or old.
- We would be betraying a deceased spouse.
- We fear competition with others our age.
- We don't think we have enough to talk about anymore.
- We don't want to make decisions.
- We can't make decisions.
- We feel anger toward women/men in general.
- We are hesitant to go out alone.
- We are no longer—or still not—interested in sex.
- We're apprehensive about how to make sex happen.
- We don't feel we have the proper attire for attracting a date.
- We don't know what to wear on a date.
- We don't know how to flirt or make small talk.
- We don't have time.
- We haven't emotionally healed since our last relationship.
- We want to lose some weight first.
- We are put off by the amount of effort required for dating.
- We are afraid of hurting someone else or getting hurt

ourselves.

- We simply can't be bothered.
- We feel embarrassed by our wrinkles or sagging bodies.*

*A word about plastic surgery: beware. Some people do well with it, and some do not. But either way, don't expect to look *younger*, unless you "do" every part of your body. Most who have had it may look a bit "newer" for a while, but age always catches up with us. Surgically enhanced aging people don't look younger: they look like aging people with unusually tight skin! *Note:* I may change my mind someday.

"Gorgeous" is not a good stock to invest in. No matter what you do, one day, you are going to lose everything on your investment.

— *Town and Country* magazine

To summarize, if we wish to date, we don't need a reason. But while dating, like fine wine, can be exquisite, it isn't for everyone. So if you are expecting me to talk you into dating, stop reading right now and pass this guide along to a friend.

There's nothing wrong with taking a stand against dating unless you are not being honest with yourself. Excuses are not acceptable if you would secretly like to enjoy another's company. If this describes you, I suggest that you read on and learn, in the company of others who share your feelings.

Every once in a while, something or someone comes along to scramble your preconceptions. Keep your mind open, and be ready to discover new truths about yourself. Then, whatever you find, follow your pleasure.

EAT LIKE YOU MEAN IT

Few things can make us feel as lonely as does eating alone, particularly in a restaurant. And few things are as nurturing as sharing a meal, either at home or in a restaurant. One of the earliest ways our parents calmed and satisfied us was through food. My husband and I frequently laughed that our best conversations took place over restaurant food. Do I have to remind you about the eating scene in the 1963 movie *Tom Jones,* when Tom and his Rubenesque lover fed one another turkey legs and succulent fruits, sans napkins? I'm still perspiring.

The point is that eating out together is something akin to sleeping together: it's great when it's good!

Don't behave like a shrinking violet when asked to join someone in this sensuous, or at least delightful, endeavor. Show some enthusiasm and some appetite.

As I was enjoying brunch with one of my sons recently, he watched me intently. "You really love to eat, don't you?"

he asked, looking perplexed. "Most women just pick, but you eat with such enthusiasm—it's really great."

We like to see each other happy. It's true, when a man takes a woman to dinner, he likes to see her eat. While the reverse is also true, traditionally men almost always eat well. History, however, shows that beginning in the nineteenth century, women would eat at home before going out with a man in order to appear delicate and frugal. Those days are over. Eating together is fun, so enjoy it.

Don't be afraid to make menu suggestions or offer an opinion. If you don't, the other person has to all the work. So when you are asked what you want to eat, *say something.* (If you are asked what movie you would like to see, *say something.* You can always rent *Tom Jones.*) If your date doesn't like your suggestion, he or she can speak up!

Note: Watch your alcohol consumption. Not only can it make you look bad, but it also clouds your judgment. You want to be able to assess the evening fairly.

I believe we are all secretly happy we can't figure our relationships out. It keeps our minds working. I think we have to be grateful for the one thing in our lives that keeps us from being totally focused on eating.

— Jerry Seinfeld

KNOW THYSELF

Be honest. Even when your date suggests an activity, you are not obliged to agree. You want to join your date in something that you, too, enjoy doing and something you would enjoy discussing afterward.

The first date is likely to be the least comfortable date you will have with that person. Don't pretend to like doing something you hate. Don't try to do something you cannot do. For instance, unless you both have done it before, beware of sports like sky diving, surfing, bungee jumping, or motorcycling. The danger level is high for young people, and the safety factor is likely to be more of a concern with age. Plus, you may get helmet hair!

Even going to the opera may be risky if you're with a Rolling Stones fan!

It's easier to share in the decision-making when you know what your own interests are. If you aren't sure, think about what your friends like to do with you. Why do they seek you out for that activity? Does your presence make it more enjoyable for them? If you are not sure, listen to the compliments people bestow upon you. Sometimes there's a hint in them.

"Know thyself." What qualities do *you* like about yourself? Display these qualities when you are meeting someone new. And remember them when you are feeling anxious and/or unattractive.

Getting to know yourself *and* someone new, concurrently, can be a little nerve-wracking.

But you can do this.

Whatever you can do or dream you can do, begin it. Boldness has genius, power and magic in it.

— Johannes von Goethe

FIRST DATE DO'S

To get that first date, decide who looks interesting to you. Then try the following:

- Smile at someone who interests you. But don't let your smile linger.
- If the situation permits, chat briefly.
- After the smile and/or the comments, turn your attention somewhere else. You may have to actually excuse yourself. If you are not sure what to say, just say, "It was nice speaking with you" and move on. Thus, you are giving the person the opportunity to think about how pleasant you were, or look, or how nice it was to have an encounter with you, however briefly.
- When someone is interested, in most cases she or he

will find a way to be with you again. If that doesn't happen, consider it a trial run.

- If you meet again or bump into one another, accidentally or on purpose, mention something about the last time you met. This lets the person know that you were paying attention to that previous conversation.

- Make sure that person knows your name. If it hasn't been mentioned already, you can be the one to end the encounter, by saying, "My name is Blossom Flowers (or Dennis Tennis), and I thoroughly enjoyed our conversation." Hopefully, that person will respond in kind and reveal his or her name. But if not, and if you receive a call from an unknown suitor, make certain that you immediately establish how you know one another.

- Once you have met and the encounter has passed, don't obsess over it. Either the other person will make the next move or you will. It may take a week, a day, or a month or more. Don't agonize. Don't even wait. Keep living your life.

- Once a connection is established, *don't fixate* on how it's going to end—or when. It will or it won't end as you wish! But not to worry—it's either a good time or a good story.

Note: If being with someone gives you an uneasy feeling, regarding his or her demeanor or motive, trust your instinct and end the date politely. And end the communication permanently.

Life is a rush into the unknown. You can duck down and hope nothing hits you.

Or stand up as tall as you can, show your teeth, and say, "BRING IT ON, BABY, AND DON'T BE STINGY WITH THE JALAPEÑOS!"

> — Fireman's Fund Insurance ad
> *Architectural Digest*

DECISIONS, DECISIONS

Decide to behave in ways that spark another person's interest. For example, gentle, flattering attention makes you most attractive, as does intermittent reinforcement. Don't be afraid to be attentive or to receive attention. You may have to nudge yourself a bit, but contrary to what you may think, it's not hokey. You are not a fake. What you are doing may simply be unfamiliar to you, so it feels a bit unnatural.

Do it anyway.

At our ripe ages, we don't want to worry much about age differences. Personality differences and differences of interests, beliefs, or values are much more significant. However, there are things that become easier when we are within 10 or so years of one another, such as feeling more comfortable with each other's families or more physically or sexually comfortable. Of course, nature has its own ideas and sometimes, even when there is apparent compatibility in all areas, someone becomes incapacitated in ways that affect the relationship and the compatibility. It is still helpful to seek a comfort level initially in as many areas as possible.

If you find someone you wish to date, be willing to give the dating a chance. Don't get too serious too quickly. First, learn all you can about the other person . . . and learn about yourself *with* that person.

Give yourself a choice. Date long enough to get to know *several* people. Be aware of how you respond to various personalities. It's not only important to know who you are with others, their friends, and their family, but it's important to see who they are with you, your friends, and your family. You both should be thinking.

Avoid attributing the course of your life to *fate.*

Focus on friendship first. No matter how "right" it seems, your date is someone you have just met. She/he is a virtual stranger. So be smart. Be responsible. Stay tuned in.

It's most important to listen carefully to *everything* your date says about himself/herself. Don't *miss* any negative signals. Don't *overlook* the signals you receive. Don't *rationalize away* a prospect's negative traits. And don't *apologize* for them.

Don't *excuse* bad behavior. *Run* from aggressiveness and anger *as fast as you can.* If you remember nothing else that I have said, remember this paragraph. It will not only assure you of a beautiful dating experience: it could *save your life.*

You may make some mistakes in judgment. That is expected. But don't compromise your principles, and don't change who you truly are because of those mistakes. Don't try to be what you think someone else is looking for. As soon as you do, you can be assured that the other person's requirements will change. Remember that *your* requirements may change as well.

Always be a first-rate version of yourself, instead of a second-rate version of someone else.
— Judy Garland

MYTH CONCEPTIONS

Some dating notions just aren't true. Worse, they tend to isolate us from what we really want. I think we often incorporate them into our own philosophies in order to protect ourselves from hurt.

Here are several of those misconceptions:

Men die sooner than women, so for the maturing woman, there aren't enough good men. Not true. Perhaps good men/women take more time to identify, and you must be more diligent and discerning. But if you visit "appropriate" venues, where there are likely to be "appropriate" people, and you are open and receptive to conversation, you are likely to meet someone, even if she/he is not "the" one.

By this time in our lives, we have been too hurt to care about trying again. It is unfortunate that some of us have had bad examples for mates. But if our goal is to meet someone and experience a loving relationship, we can repair the earlier damage. It may take more work. And more time.

Older dating hopefuls can't beat the odds. We don't know how much we know. And as we mature, our memories play tricks on us. But we do, wittingly or unwittingly, assimilate that which we have learned about life during our younger years and often, our not-single years. So now that we have learned, we will be more organized and informed. We will have a plan. Right? And this will give us an edge. And even if we don't beat the odds, we may gain a friendship.

The worst thing that can happen will happen. The *worst* thing that could happen is that you give up. You might simply try to make friends with someone. If this is the result of your attempt to find a date, is it so bad?

You can only love one person per lifetime. If you have lost a loved one, that person cannot be replaced. But every love is different. And there are so many kinds of relationships. So while it's true that we can't actually replace a love, we can certainly love again. No one has ever measured how much love our hearts can hold.

This person would be great for someone else, but not for me. This may or may not be true. New people have new attributes and qualities. They may not be the traits you are used to, but don't be quick to cast people aside! Speak to a number of people. Begin by looking for what is "right," right now. Allow your future to evolve. Robert Frost, in his poem "The Mending Wall," said that before he built a wall, he would ask what he was "walling in" and what he was "walling out."

You have to be young to date. Check out the senior Internet sites and, if you are not adept at the computer, read the personals in print media. Hopefuls are still reaching out in their seventies, eighties, and even into their nineties. I repeat: forget about age differences. Years of experience and growth are great levelers. Don't let anyone convince you otherwise.

All of the available older men/women are losers. Stop looking for perfection! Start looking for quality. But be vigilant in detecting destructive behaviors. Beware of getting your head (and good judgment) turned around by wealth, education, "good family," impressive careers, fancy cars, designer clothes, and even spotless reputations. Look beyond these arbitrary trappings. Don't discount the diamonds in the rough.

There are so many crazy people running around masked as "normal." Don't needlessly scare yourself about deviants. Frightening yourself about molesters, alcoholics, fortune hunters, and such will keep your focus on the negative. Think of each meeting as an opportunity to *find out* what you are dealing with. Looking in appropriate venues, taking your time, and even interviewing your prospective dates are paramount. Be cognizant of clues. And try not to become emotionally involved too soon.

(Fill in the blank) has ruined my dating experience forever. You don't have to recreate your history. If this is your pattern, a good therapist can set you right fairly quickly. We can become conditioned to attract another person's character flaws, and often, those flaws are the same as our own. This can feel easy and comfortable for a while, but will come back to bite us. A simple way to handle dysfunction is to flat out *reject it!*

I feel too old to date. Too much time has passed. It's not possible to feel close again. I have lumped together these excuses that weaken in the face of this universal truth: Most of us deal with insecurities, especially when considering re-dating after an extended commitment or hiatus. Some of us just hide it better than others do!

Here is a technique that will relax you when you are feeling apprehensive about re-dating. When visiting a meeting place frequented by others wishing to connect socially, begin conversing with one or several people with whom you feel comfortable. This nonsexual, nonthreatening gesture will calm you enough to allow you to be receptive to someone in whom you may be interested.

Challenge what you suspect are myths.

The real voyage of discovery consists, not in seeing new landscapes, but in having new eyes.

— Marcel Proust
Remembrance of Things Past

UGH . . . NO BARS, PLEASE

Potential dating candidates who don't want to frequent bars may use these excuses: "I don't drink," "I can't tolerate the noise," and "I don't enjoy dealing with, or being around, inebriated people." Well, I don't like these things either. Therefore, I've devised a list of venues where one may meet a prospective date or would be likely at least to meet a person worthy of a conversation. Remember—an initial encounter is only about the moment. Don't overthink it.

Here is my list of alternatives to the bar scene. At the very least, you may have an interesting time . . . actually enjoy yourself . . . and learn something new!

- **Computer classes**—Be a savvy "techie" (and impress the grandchildren).
- **Special interest groups**—Everyone enjoys *something.*

Really.

- **Ballroom dancing lessons**—Drop a pound and meet a prospect.
- **Contra or folk dancing**—Not just for hippies anymore.
- **Local sightseeing cruises**—Set your sights on *all* of the sights.
- **Museum tours**—Artifacts may not be the only things on exhibit.
- **Conferences, lectures, seminars**—Learn and *look.*
- **Vocal groups, choirs**—Lift up *your* voice in thanksgiving.
- **Pottery or other art classes for beginners**—Great places to meet, maybe through gregarious grandchildren.
- **Avenue, gallery walks, openings**—Create an acquaintance . . . and a masterpiece.
- **Outdoor cafés**—When weather is conducive to painted toes and "man shorts."
- **Coffee houses**—The destination depends upon your generation.
- **Art fairs**—Comfort's the word, but lose the gladiator sandals.

- **Sporting events**—Yes, you would *love* to see the team play.
- **Tennis, golf, or *any* sports-related classes**—Can result in image of hero worship.
- **Antique shops**—Not just for grandma and grandpa anymore.
- **Small town or village exploration**—Could lead to a fabulous weekend.
- **Opera, ballet, concerts, live theater**—May result in lovely intermezzos.
- **Home entertaining**—Ask guests to bring a friend whom no one else knows—yet.
- **Evening university classes**—May lead to dinner before class.
- **Travel and tours**—Stop for a snack . . . in Tuscany.
- **Auctions**—You may find something, or *someone*, worth a lot.
- **Play-reading groups**—Perfect for acting out romantic love scenes.
- **Support groups**—Hand-holding heaven.
- **Book stores**—You never know what, or whom, you'll find among the stacks.
- **Book clubs**—Be an intellectual . . . or just look like

one.

- **Synagogues or churches**—From whence your help may *really* come.

- **Indoor and outdoor food markets**—Play dumb . . . get help feeling the melons.

- **Walk a pet**—Dogs and chinchillas walk, but cats must be dragged.

- **Health clubs**—Men like sweat. Women don't. Act accordingly.

- **Cooking classes**—Cook up something hot.

- **Wine tastings**—Enjoy a date with a variety of varietals.

- **Card clubs**—Know when to hold 'em and, well, when to *hold* 'em.

- **Singles events**—Know your audience.

- **Video rental stores**—Get there before they become obsolete!

- **Internet dating sites**—Age-specific (Can they legally do that?)

- **Newspaper/magazine personals**—Chuckle, then choose.

- **Reunions**—Network the heck out of 'em. Sometimes they lead to unions.

- **Personal introductions**—Don't sweat these . . . they're not likely to happen!
- **Neighborhood walks**—If no luck, head for the nearest chocolate.
- **Swim clubs**—Not for the faint of heart.
- **Public socials and dances**—Dance as though *everyone* is watching!

Let it be duly noted that bars are still the venue of choice for many re-daters-to-be and have been known to spawn innumerable fine relationships!

If I took my time, sampled every possibility, eventually I'd hit on the perfect combination and come into my own.

— Michael Dorris
A Yellow Raft in Blue Water

EASIER TO BEAR

Here are some things you can do to assure an easier dating experience:

Don't call dating "dating" if the word is anxiety producing. Pick a code name for it, like "bird watching" or "ham hunting." Call it anything but "*dating.*"

Do what you enjoy. That way, if you don't meet anyone, you will still have a good time.

Drive your own car. Whether you are meeting friends or a new date, you'll have the freedom to leave any time you wish. This takes some of the pressure off if you are unhappy for any reason. Among other unpleasantries, you may be bored, overwhelmed, uncomfortable, tired, ill, or having second thoughts about remaining. You may sense that something is amiss with regard to your date. Leave before anything gets to you!

If you go out with more than one friend, know that you are less likely to meet someone. Most people are unlikely to approach a group of strangers.

If you have not met anyone at any of the places you are accustomed to frequenting for that purpose, change your venue. Use the list in the previous chapter! Or change the time that you usually go. But in any case, break with the familiar.

Go somewhere you have not gone before. Take courage. There's help everywhere.

Ask everyone you know whether they know someone to whom you might be introduced. There are people who will be happy to introduce you if they do know someone. And there are people who are hoping to be introduced to someone like you. But you have to be proactive in getting the project in gear. Ask your doctor. Ask your nail tech. Ask your neighbors. Ask anyone who knows you. Ask the UPS man. Just don't ask him out—he's mine.

Your smile is your insurance plan. If the person who interests you shares your interest but doesn't know what to do about it, your smile will clinch the deal. It's the nicest part of a face, at any age. Smile, smile, smile!

We must always meet each other with a smile. For it is the smile that is the beginning of love.

— Mother Teresa

Life is like a schoolroom. Every relationship is a lesson. After so many years, you are probably an apt learner. Work on earning extra credit!

If you keep someone talking, you have made a friend. This is how it works. The more you can encourage people to talk about *themselves,* the more they will feel they like *you.* If you ask people questions about themselves, you will make it even easier for *them* to talk because *you* have done the work of creating the subject matter. But be forewarned: The older we are, the more we have to say. So it could mean a long evening! And you may have to wait for the relationship to begin before you get to talk about *you.*

The best dentist in the world is difficult to bear. Getting rid of the stuffed animals of your childhood is difficult to bear. Not realizing you left your keys on the piano until you are standing at your car in two feet of snow is difficult to bear. Running out of chocolate is difficult to bear. Dating, by comparison, is a piece of cake. Approach it with anticipation! Have it with ice cream!

Life is a banquet and most poor suckers are starving to death.

— Jerome Lawrence and Robert Edwin Lee, *Auntie Mame*

DATING IS SCARY

Are you still feeling scared?

Dating *can* be scary, and here are two of the common reasons this is true:

You can't control it, because it's in two people's hands. (Sometimes more.)

You don't know how, or when, or if the ensuing relationship will end.

There are some things we simply can't control. We can't control the direction our dating will take. We can't control the other person. The fact is that we can only control ourselves—and that's only *some* of the time! Accept it and let go of the control you only *think* you have.

We can never experience the end of something until we are there. We can, however, experience *apprehension* regarding the ending. And if this stymies us so severely that we avoid dating altogether, we will be *guaranteed* an *unhappy* ending.

Security is mostly a superstition. It does not exist in nature. Life is either a daring adventure, or it's nothing.

— Helen Keller, *The Open Door*

Sure, there *are* some dating potholes, but with some smart self-conversation, we can avert disaster.

There are those of us who fear the date itself. True, some of the prospective dates you meet may seem strange to you and may, in fact, *be* strange. Some of the experiences you share with a date may be off-putting and uncomfortable to address. These kinds of circumstances are surmountable by using common sense. Unless you are being restrained—which makes it not a dating but rather a hostage situation—you can, literally, walk away from whatever scares you.

My dear Polish grandmother, in her broken English, put any catastrophe that befell her into perspective with the exclamation "Suz vut!"— her interpretation of "So what!"

So if an unexpected catastrophe befalls *your* relationship, even though you have been safe and logical in your choice of dates, simply respond to it with a "Suz vut!"

And if that's not enough to stave off the anxiety, add "What is the *worst* thing that could possibly happen?" (My sister the therapist taught me this one.)

You'll find your answer to be much less frightening than your fear! You may end up shaking your head in disbelief at your fate, but you'll be doing it with half a smile! And you won't be afraid to try again. The only failure is failing to act.

After all, the secret of walking on water is knowing where the stones are.

You must do the thing you think you cannot do.

— Eleanor Roosevelt

MOURNING, AND HOW TO UNDO IT

Mourning is not just for death any more. Any person who has left one or more relationships behind, for any reason, has experienced a sort of mourning. A long hiatus between dating partners allows space for this feeling to grow.

Curiously, the feelings associated with mourning can persist, no matter what the circumstances were that terminated the relationship. At *any* age, when relationships die, even relatively short relationships, one's hopes and dreams can die, too. And with them die possibilities.

It is thought-provoking that this emotionally charged state may exist *even when the relationship was a bad one!*

That's because, bad or good, you have lost a partner. If you already have an issue with abandonment, whether as a result of conditions during childhood or those associated with aging and loneliness, therapy can often help. There are help groups for such circumstances as well.

If we are lucky enough to be mentally intact, memories don't leave us. And it is perfectly normal to remember a past partner in the middle of doing a familiar thing with someone new or . . . simply out of nowhere. These memories will probably become less frequent as you and your new partner begin building your own history together, and creating more memories of your own. You won't forget those memories you choose to keep of a past love. The good memories will remain in your heart and will support you as you navigate the uncertain waters of dating again. And you'll be happy to replace the bad ones!

Let us be of good cheer, remembering that the misfortunes hardest to bear are those which never come.

— Amy Lowell

IRRESISTIBLY AVAILABLE

To be irresistible, you have to be young, firm, thin, rich, powerful, good-looking, and experienced. WRONG! In actuality, you can be irresistible at any age and without any of these characteristics. The key is to be *willing*—and even eager—to date. Even if you are old, saggy, plump, of modest means, have no professional status, and don't feel attractive— if you are *enthusiastic, optimistic, and available,* you can be irresistible.

Here is the *real* formula. To be irresistible to others, *let go of the resistance you have to them!*

This being said, there are specific ways to appear *receptive*:

Focus on what you do want and not on what you don't want. If you don't know what you want, it's time to begin figuring it out. Because if you don't know what you want, how can you go about finding it? Remember the Cheshire Cat's bad advice?

In the same vein, think about the pleasant time you want to have and not about what you are afraid *might* happen. Richard Bach, in his book *Illusions*, says, "Argue for your limitations and they're yours!"

Focus on the *quality* of people and not on their physical, social, or professional traits—neither the positive nor the negative ones.

"Love thyself."

That season of love that you've been looking for is already in your your heart. Right now, someone you know is looking everywhere for it—and it's in *you*.

— *Peyton Place*, 1957 film

GET OUT OF SINGLES EVENTS

Many singles find singles events distasteful. Unless an event is built around an interesting activity, we feel like a bunch of desperate people with nothing in common. Except loneliness. So should we continue to attend them?

Yes, absolutely. But we have to understand what we are getting into when we do. There actually *is* a phenomenon called "lonely desperation." As we age, in particular, we feel undeservedly that "this" one will be our last chance. And it shows on our faces, in our eyes, and in our conversation—or lack of it.

Remember when I said that going out with a group of friends can be off-putting to someone wanting to approach you, or to another in your party? Here is the exception.

Attending a singles event is the time when you *do* want

to go with friends, and preferably friends with whom you would generally enjoy yourself anyway.

If going to singles events, with or without friends, saddens you because it makes you feel lonely in a crowd, then don't attend them. Stick to activities that you can enjoy, even if you don't meet anyone new. But before you give singles activities up completely, look for the humor in them and try one more time. With the right attitude, they *can* be confidence boosters.

The image of truth changes, depending on the color of the light.

— *Eve's Bayou*, 1997 film

GO TO PARTIES

It's best never to miss a party if you can help it. Every guest has something to offer. It's a numbers game, so plan to meet as many people as possible.

Once at the party, tell everyone you know and everyone you meet that you are interested in meeting others. There are many matchmakers around.

But be warned. While you are trying to meet new friends, don't neglect your old friends. They are your support system and more resourceful than your local library!

Networking is your key to success.

If you know your host/hostess well, you might suggest having everyone bring a single friend to the party. If space and additional food are no object, more single guests would probably be welcomed.

Even if you are only going to a coffee café, invite others.

Friends and friends of friends can offer you new experiences. Ask them about where to go and what to do. I promise that you will leave with more possibilities than you came with.

Enjoy this time of freedom! Have fun with it!

Romance is made to be enjoyed, not endured.

— *Dogs*, 1976 film

GO MINDFULLY

When you meet or are introduced to someone, one of the most self-destructive things you can do is to try to second-guess what that person thinks or feels about you. It is important to stay focused on what *you* think and feel.

And here is why:

Try as you may, there *is* no way to second-guess what another person is thinking or feeling about anything. Therefore, attempting to do so wastes your time.

I've read that we should "stay behind our own eyes." And if we stay behind our own eyes, we can gather the information we need to decide who is best for us.

You cannot live your life looking at yourself from someone else's point of view.

— *Vogue* photo shoot

RULES RULE

One notable thing about dating again is that it's not *very* different from the way it used to be! And you *remember* how it used to be, right? Let's revisit the rules, just in case you've forgotten something.

Never go out without money or a credit card.

Refuse to go to a lonely, empty, or dangerous spot.

Never invite a first date past your front door.

Any date who initially courts you through expensive meals, tickets, or gifts and such, *may* want something in return. Be alert to what that is. Ask! And if you don't want the same thing, end the association then and there. Be very firm and definitive.

Whoever initiates the date does the paying, unless something else is agreed upon. If prior agreement would be more comfortable for you, then discuss it with your date before you go out.

Always use condoms when you are pursuing sexual intimacy. AIDS numbers are diminishing worldwide, but rising among those over age 55! *We are not immune to sexual diseases of any kind.*

If your date shows signs of having had too much alcohol, then you should stop drinking and insist that you drive home. If you do not drive or do not drive at night, any restaurant or bar will call a transportation service for you. Once home, decide whether it is worth going through this every time the two of you go out, and make a choice. (Uncontrollable drinking always is best dealt with professionally.)

Recreational drugs, and those who use them, should be avoided like the plague.

Turn your cell phone to the silent mode. Keep it with you. Know exactly where you put it. Don't leave it at home or in the car.

If we did all the things we are capable of doing, we would literally astound ourselves.

— Thomas A. Edison

DON'T BE CRUEL

Rejection happens. And there's only one thing you absolutely *have* to remember about it.

Rejection is not about you! It is about the other person's preferences and perspectives. Try not to personalize it.

Unfortunately, some people just don't call us back. Some people are just not that "into" us. This happens to men and women, at every age. "Suz vut!"

Not calling back may even be a compliment. Some people may be spooked by having too good a time with someone. Some people are simply afraid of commitment. For some, success is also scary. Some people are afraid they can't sustain a relationship. They're usually the one-night-standers!

There are other fish in the sea, aren't there?

As King Arthur's manservant observed in *Camelot,* "There

are an immeasurable number of *drops* in the sea, Sir, but some of the drops *sparkle*!" Hold out for the date that sparkles. But don't stop fishing.

The only real risk in life is not taking one. Don't waste your time fretting about the one that got away.

When God closes one door, he always opens another. Even if sometimes it's *hell in the hallway*!
— Unknown

COME A LITTLE CLOSER

Intimacy . . . *yes*! This is what it's all about! *Isn't it?*

But intimacy does test us.

We all learn, as we recover from a first date, that we are emotionally fragile. And clumsy. We hurt each other when we don't mean it. It's been happening since we were teenagers. In today's world, it may happen even earlier.

The closer we get as a couple, the more we become vulnerable to being hurt.

This is how intimacy can "get" us.

Here is something you might try to help alert you to potential problems with intimacy in *your* relationship. Talk about your own secrets (without betraying anyone you know).

And ask your date some conversational questions about relationships . . . questions that hopefully will draw out the secrets. If your date is open to sharing, pay attention to what things went wrong in previous relationships. *Pay attention!* History, without help, repeats itself.

The point of this exercise is to be alert to differences and to similarities. If you are aware early enough, you may be able to avert problems. Note, too, what things were good . . . and keep in the forefront those things that *are* good.

Here are some things you can do to nurture your intimacy:

Try to establish some kind of pleasant sexual communication.

Life happens. Happily celebrate the good stuff and those things you have survived together.

Things are often difficult. Try to resolve your disappointments. Comfort each other when times are painful. Be kind to one another. And then be kinder.

Play together. Share some secrets. Devise some clandestine signals between you, such as special smiles and touches.

Forgive one another.

Pain and beauty, our constant bedfellows.

— Nick Bantock, *Griffin & Sabine: An Extraordinary Correspondence*

NOT *MY* DATING QUIZ

I cannot take credit for this quiz. I tore it out of a publication many years ago. Testing yourself is lots of fun and may surprise you as well! I know I learned a few things.

All of the answers follow all of the questions. Here goes:

QUESTIONS

- What are the top three things that men say attract them to a woman?
- What are the top three things that women say attract them to a man?
- Which of the five senses (Sight, smell, hearing, taste, touch) is the most powerful in attraction?
- If you were going to whisper sweet nothings in someone's ear, in which ear are you likely to whisper them?

- Which are the two phrases that women most want to hear?
- What are the words that men most want to hear?
- What do both women *and* men want to hear?
- What is the best way to get someone to go out with you or go home with you?
- Where is the best place to meet someone?
- How many approaches should you make before you give up on a dating prospect?
- What is the best way to show someone you are interested?
- How can you tell someone is interested in you?
- How much eye contact should you engage in when you are interested in someone?
- What are two good ways to deal with rejection?
- How many dates are recommended before you know someone is "the one?"
- What is a good test of true love?
- What are three qualities that make for the best lasting relationship?
- What is the most important rule about using a condom?
- Why do some men roll over and go to sleep after sex?

ANSWERS

- "Looks" first, then "a good personality," "intelligence," and "sense of humor," in that order. Many men include "eyes."

- "Personality" ("warmth," "caring"), first and then, "trustworthiness" ("honesty"), "intelligence," and "sense of humor," in that order. Many women include "eyes." When women talk about the subject in greater detail, they mention "money."

- Smell. Messages go straight and, therefore, quickly, from the olfactory bulb to the brain. Many people also say "sight."

- You would want to whisper into the left ear, which connects to the right side of the brain, which is the romantic side (where the romantic feelings are initiated).

- Women want to hear "I love you" and "You are beautiful." They often joke about things relating to money, such as wanting to hear a man say, "My credit card is platinum!"

- Men want to hear how good they are, including in bed. In a survey, some answers were "Let's get naked," "I don't want a commitment," "The football game is on," and "Let *me* pay!"

- Both women and men want to hear "I love you" and their name.
- The best way "to pick someone up" is to be natural and be you. Survey answers included "Look and listen" and "Smile."
- Go where you feel comfortable—or go where energy is palpable (sporting events, amusement parks, concerts). I've given you a list of other places in the earlier chapter "UGH, NO BARS, PLEASE."
- Make three approaches before you give up.
- Show them by admitting it, being very complimentary, and making eye contact. And smile a lot!
- Check out your date's body language, his/her eye contact, and whether she/he seems to really want to talk to you.
- Make eye contact for at least 60 percent of the time.
- First, switch your attention to that which makes you feel good, and second, realize that people have different batting averages. Be positive and optimistic!
- Follow a six-date minimum.
- Going through crises together.
- The top three answers: commitment, communication, caring.

- Condom-sense means using protection *every* time you engage in sex.
- After sex, men may *be* tired or may have trained themselves to be. Others want to escape intimacy.

Please note: While I did change some of the words above for clarity or simplicity, I did not change any of the answers. But that doesn't mean they are always true, or true for *you.* Instinct, intelligence, individuality, and your own history can affect every answer.

Everything you are is everything you need. All you have to do is show up.

— Jerry Lewis

WHO KNEW?

Various *assumptions* clutter our path to dating success, no matter how old we are. We hear things (as on television), see things, and are told things (by friends, media, etc.) that skew our thinking, causing us to believe there is some sort of "ideal" we should be searching for . . . someone who is "meant" for us.

What we forget, or perhaps don't realize, is that the idea of marriage was *not* originally based upon love. The institution of marriage was created in order to pass down land through families, without complications or question, and to keep workers home on the farm.

Too, the concept of "forever" has been altered by advanced medical and health techniques and breakthroughs. People used to live until they were, maybe, 30. "Forever" was a fairly short hop.

In bygone days, all energies were focused on working the land together. The woman cooked and cleaned, and birthed and cared for children. The man hunted for food and protected the family. Marriage was more of a business proposition than anything else. That was, basically, the *only* kind of relationship. Most people only knew their own family and few others, all of whom lived close by. So no one had many choices. You were married or you weren't.

Picking a lifetime mate was a means to ensure survival. The commitment was to last forever, and any resulting romance was a plus.

Relationships of every type and variety abound today. We deal with differences in color, creed, heritage, language, religion, sexual preference, and age, which have the potential to present stumbling blocks. So it's a bit more difficult to maintain a relationship than it used to be. Relationships today may last 50 or 60 years, or more. But often . . . they don't last at all.

One question may be, "Do we harbor notions that hinder our ability to nurture and maintain such complex relationships?" I think we do. I think we need to rethink some of the things we believe and pay attention to, so that *our* relationships can last "forever," if we're seeking "forever," *and* be stoked by romance and sex.

I'd like to share some of the notions that I feel need reconsidering:

The mass media floods us with portrayals of idealized romance and romantic ideals. Most of us would say that they do not affect us personally. But when I see how we pour over glamour and movie star magazines . . . and how we cram into plastic surgeons' offices . . . and how we squeeze into the styles foisted upon us by retail buyers, I have to wonder. And you should wonder, too. Just how many of the images and ideas we espouse can be directly traced to mass media hype?

> What makes a woman beautiful? Is it the way she looks . . . or the way she looks at the world?
>
> — Oil of Olay ad

We often seek a person who fits our ideal. "I know what I want" is a badge of definitive and assured thinking. But it can sabotage us. While realizing we cannot expect the ideal, we need to find someone whose characteristics appeal to us. This sounds like a no-brainer, and yet I've heard, "I know what I want" from one "independent" person after another. If you *know what you want* and spend your time looking only for that ideal, you are going to miss a bunch of nice surprises!

> I *prefer* a life of surprises.
>
> — Marc Chagall

There's such a thing as "love at first sight." Perhaps. But only if you are referring to how you feel about someone's appearance. You can love a suit or someone's hands at first sight, or even a person's demeanor. But how much can you really know about what's inside?

> I try to believe in six impossible things, every day, before breakfast.
>
> — Lewis Carroll
> *Alice in Wonderland*

Absence makes the heart grow fonder. Hmmmm. Unless

someone is having a terrible time being away from you and begging you to come back, that someone *can* do without you. "Out of sight" usually ends up being "out of mind." Sometimes, under a special set of circumstances as when two totally committed people have jobs in different cities, this works. But it's a good idea to date where you live.

As long as you get there before it's over, you're not too late.

— James J. Walker

A good woman's nurturing and faithfulness can change a "beast" into a "beauty" of a man. I don't think so. No one can change us. We can only change ourselves. And we can never change anyone else. I'm serious. Don't even try it. It's a waste of time.

My one regret in life is that I am not someone else.

— Woody Allen

If you love each other, having different values doesn't matter. If you don't share values, I am wondering what it is you love. Give that some thought. If you like different foods or movies, that's one thing. You can alternate types of restaurants or movies. But if you suspect you have different values, and you think it doesn't matter, you'd better do a lot of talking before you begin to raise a child. Or a grandchild.

Saying "I love you" is a conversation, not a message.

— *Difficult Conversations: How to Talk about What Matters Most*

Destiny or fate brings you to your perfect partner. Let me know, after seven months of dating, whether or not you still believe your dating partner is perfect. I'm laughing. Destiny and fate are laughing too.

When fickle fate pitches you a curve ball, it is actually a chance to learn how to dance on a shifting carpet.

— *Bazaar* magazine

I think you get what I am saying. Things change. Times change. People change. Relationships change. You will not be able to keep up with the changes, nor will you be receptive to them if you are hanging on to preconceived notions.

Marriages and relationships just aren't what they "used to be." And maybe they never were.

LET'S GET PERSONAL

In the past, I intermittently flirted with the "Personals" ads in the newspaper, basically for amusement. But then I started meeting singles of diverse ages who, through this rather outdated search method, had met some pretty neat people. This gave me a bit more respect for the "Personals" method of screening and meeting. I grew increasingly curious about how *many* people in *my* age range, and older, use this form of social connection as their primary method of arranging dates. I also wondered about the ages of those who were "advertising." So I decided to conduct some research.

I was living in Delray, Florida, at this point in my research, and I used the Palm Beach *Post* column titled "The Meeting Post." (Florida is a perfect place to do a study of the behavior of aging singles.)

First I did a statistical breakdown by age, without designating gender, as I was concerned primarily with the relationship between the ages of the more mature souls who were still bravely "putting themselves out there," and the number of ads they placed.

My biggest surprise came when I began reading the ads themselves. Clearly, older singles conveyed as much optimism, self-appreciation, and positive self-image as younger ones. In fact, if I removed the actual age reference, it was virtually impossible for me to guess the age of the writer.

I looked at 200 entries in all. And again, my statistics are not broken down into female/male categories.

Here is what I found:

Ages 55–60—19 entries

Ages 60–70—61 entries

Ages 70+—16 entries

No stated age—9 entries (I used these as they were seeking men over 65.)

In other words:

Nearly half of all entrants were 55+.

Well over one-fourth of the entrants were 60+.

And those 70+ made a very respectable showing:

95 out of 200 were 55.

61 out of 200 were 60+.

16 out of 200 were 70+.

You don't have to spend a fortune every month on the Internet. The old-fashioned ways of finding dates still work!

Now, a word about the Internet. Internet dating is expensive. Many people cannot afford it. Many don't have the time for it. (It takes a lot of time to search this way.) Many are not computer savvy, and some don't even own a computer. And many are fearful of perceived dangers.

For these reasons, I recommend at least checking out the newspaper dating columns. I must admit they are fun to read, and the finest, most respected newspapers in the country print them.

As names are never printed in these columns, I'll share some real ads with you, eliminating the newspaper identification numbers but stating the ages of the "advertisers." Otherwise, *I have not changed one word*! As we traditionally think, "but we are too old" when we resist actively searching for companionship in this fashion, I have chosen ads written by those who clearly *aren't*! Ignore the age given, and I challenge you to be able to guess what it is!

"Sexy senior, F (female), 75, 5 ft. 4 in., blonde/blue, full-figured, wants to meet personable, intelligent senior, 70–80,

5 ft.+, few extra pounds OK. N/S (no smoking), personality and chemistry important. Must have learned how not to "sweat the small stuff." I'm affectionate, spontaneous, have a great personality, love traveling, dogs, cruising, movies, theater, bingo, and gambling. How about you?"

"Happy, outgoing, good-natured F, 81, enjoys movies, dancing, shows, walks, much more. Looking for an easy-going, warm-hearted, simple gentleman who enjoys life's little pleasures."

"Slim male, 80, loves playing golf and bridge, dancing, travel, theater, dining, and bowling. Seeking attractive lady with similar interests, 66–75, caring and thoughtful, to share long-term relationship."

"Looking for elderly gentleman to share good times, attractive woman, 90, good health, very active, enjoys bridge and dancing. Let's meet over a cup of coffee. Call me."

"Male, 75, honest, very active, emotionally/financially secure, looking for a companion who is tired of being alone, 66–76."

"Male, 80, 5 ft. 10 in., 210 lbs., retired military veteran, enjoys quiet conversation, lunch/dinners out, togetherness. Seeking nice woman, low-keyed, easygoing, conversationalist, 75–82, to share the good life."

I think you probably get my point.

Happiness makes up in height, for what it lacks in length.

— Robert Frost

DEAR CYBERJOHN

The most important thing to know about Internet dating sites is that they are only sophisticated Introduction services. They do not get you dates . . . or anything else, and they assume no responsibilities. They are said to be time savers because you don't have to dress up and leave home to go "shopping." I suggest that you limit your research or you will find yourself online 24/7.

The Internet is only one way to meet someone. One of many. Don't keep doing it if you don't enjoy it after having given it a chance. *Note*: There are dating sites specifically for people over 50, but there is virtually no difference between them and other sites. Other sites electronically isolate seniors by allowing the searcher to select "preferences." Also, be aware that many dating sites charge automatic monthly fees, which can add up.

Knowing how to correspond on the Internet dating sites

is really important. You have to convince someone whom you have never met that you are OK. You need to convey that you are stable, safe, cautious, pleasant, bright, easy to talk to, and comfortable to be with, among other characteristics.

"I'm going to sit right down and write myself a letter" was the first line of a song written about 80 years ago, but you know, it's not a bad idea. Practice writing an email describing whatever you would want someone to know about you. And try to make it the type of email to which you would respond if it were written about someone else. All you should be hoping for, as a result of your first email, is an email in return.

In essence, you only have one chance to make a good first impression. This is because the Internet has made it possible to write to hundreds of people a week. There is always someone waiting to take your place in the queue.

There's something you need to know before you begin to reveal the truth about yourself. And it's that dating site devotees don't always tell the truth about themselves, nor do they always use current photographs! This is not to say that these people are lying. A woman weighing 150 pounds may see herself with "a few extra pounds," or, if she has just lost 50 pounds, she may see herself as of average weight or even "thin."

Too, people often display online photographs from earlier years, without indicating that fact. Perhaps that is how they truly see themselves today. Perhaps they believe that that one particular image best captures their current personality. They are not *usually* trying to trick anyone, but we may be fooled.

If you don't want to be shocked or disappointed by such things on your first date, don't be afraid to ask such questions online as, "How current is your photograph?" Or "Is that your present weight?" It's worth a moment of discomfort to ask such questions before you meet, rather than to have to control your reactions during a first date.

Another caveat: One can actually stretch the phone bantering stage to the point at which a meeting is no longer likely to happen. This is because the quipping and teasing, back and forth, is so prolonged that it *becomes the relationship* itself. Nothing more is going to happen.

Be alert to that point at which the phone conversation gets old, and be the one to force the issue if you must. There is a natural progression to nurturing a developing friendship/ relationship. There will be a point at which, if you haven't established a time to meet, the relationship becomes stagnant and one of you walks.

Here is the Internet letter I have chosen to reflect the kind of correspondence that turns phone conversations into meetings. It is a real letter written by someone I know. The writer was 62 when the letter was written, at which time the correspondent suggested that they finally meet.

Dear [person's name]:

I am definitely eager to meet you before [month], but I have been thinking that I might be more relaxed meeting you for the first time on *my* turf, rather than in [town where you live]. I think it might be more fun for one of us to be on home territory; and, although I am generally a risk taker, it feels a bit safer for that person to be me.

Would you consider making the short (I think it's only an hour flight) trip to [town] from [town] for a day or two, after your meetings? I will be happy to find a hotel/motel for you, pick you up at the airport, of course, so you won't have to rent a car. You'd have little else to worry about (unless you distrust my cooking)!

I know good restaurants, nice places to walk, etc. And you'll get to breathe some ocean air. One could do worse!

Give it some thought and let me know. And please, feel free to call me again. I really enjoyed talking with you.

P. S. Today was an extraordinary day. It almost felt like autumn and was a lovely respite from the last few weeks of heat and uncharacteristic humidity.

I am looking forward to your response.

Here is why I believe this to be such an effective Internet communique:

It is low-keyed and unemotional.

It is eager, yet restrained.

It is nonthreatening.

While the writer admits to being a risk taker, there is a clear indication of stability and alertness (letting the recipient know in a friendly way that the writer is aware of the risks).

It gives a forthright and cogent reason for desiring a plan other than the one previously suggested in a letter.

As the recipient would be paying for the trip to visit (this stipulation made clear by the writer), the writer offers to make the trip as easy as possible. Checking the distance, offering to pick up the recipient (using the writer's car and gas), and thus be the driver throughout the visit balances the gesture made by the recipient, the purchaser of the airline ticket.

The writer makes suggestions for filling the time so the recipient will not feel uncomfortable and will look forward to a pleasant time, whether or not there are sparks.

The writer gently limits the length of time the recipient will visit, thus minimizing any prolonged disappointment by either party.

Light (but not silly or sexy) humor softens any awkwardness in the negotiations.

The last sentence anchors the email and keeps it down to earth and general, thus discouraging any inappropriate ideas.

There is a natural, simple closing—the gentlest expectation with a hint of restraint softening the body of the email.

The letter is short and crisp, yet includes all the

information necessary to move forward.

But what if you want to end a correspondence instead of encouraging it?

There are kind ways to say "Thanks, but no thanks," via email. Try one of these:

"While you sound like a lovely person, I feel as though our interests are not compatible. Thank you so much for taking the time to explore them with me. I wish you the future that you wish for yourself."

An alternative closing sentence might read: "I feel certain that you will meet someone much better suited than I to fit your needs."

You might end with "It was a pleasure getting to know you."

Responses such as these will work most of the time, leaving the recipient feeling honored, respected, admired, and maybe even pumped up emotionally.

I've never regretted treating someone well.

— Bernard W. Nussbaum

THE "S" WORD

One of my sons called me to say that my granddaughter, then one month shy of 13, had intercepted my partially completed manuscript straight from his mailbox, though I had intended it for his sage perusal only. My granddaughter, at her impressionable age, had already begun reading it, and my son sat with her to read as well. (I had already explained to him that the manuscript contained nothing "edgy.")

Before my son had even begun reading, my granddaughter, shocked that Grammie would write a "sex book," was poised to point out to him each time I had used the word "sex."

The irony is that while, yes, I had used the word, it was only in conjunction with the word "opposite" or "same." The incident drew peals of laughter from me, and I made a point, as grandmothers and grandfathers do, to share the story with a few relatives and friends. Oh, all right, with *anyone* who would listen!

My cousin, after a hearty chuckle, responded to my story by asking whether I actually *had* written a chapter on sex. When I answered no, she asked, "Why not? How can you write about dating and aging without writing about sex?" Hmm . . . . right. I suppose I was assuming that by the time a person reaches my age, he or she pretty much knows what to do. But then I began to think about it, and I reconsidered.

As we age, the concept of sex—and sex itself—undergoes some pretty significant alterations. For many of us, our parts don't always function the way our brains do, and vice-versa.

Let's be honest. Whether resulting from our diminished hormones, our general health, our responsibilities, our concerns, or simply the joke that nature plays on us, we just don't think about sex so much as we used to. That is, we think about it, but we are less likely to follow through. Or we follow through but our bodies sabotage us.

And so, as I proposed earlier in this book, let's accept the premise that the rules are the same, but the circumstances have changed.

Basically, I still believe that what a couple does in private is . . . private. Sex later in life requires more patience, understanding, and creativity.

Chemical "enhancement" is relatively common but is safest when it is doctor sanctioned and monitored. Even sex itself should be doctor sanctioned if we have been, or are, ill. There are drugs to keep us hard, drugs to keep us wet, drugs to help us feel something nice. There are new "aids" being touted all the time. These methods can be pleasurable and even fun, but there is a danger in not knowing how you or your partner will react to them. Simple and old-fashioned "toys," such as vibrators, are often recommended or sanctioned by doctors.

Characteristic of our transition into maturity is that while it is still feasible to do what we desire sexually, we are more likely to give greater importance to other aspects of a person and a relationship: How someone treats us, when we are tired or ill. How it feels staying home, together, to read, enjoy the fire, watch TV, share a meal, take a walk, or simply be together. How it feels to lie in bed together, just holding hands or cuddling. How we handle a partner's need to sleep in a separate bedroom.

How much faith and trust do we have in our partner? Can we be assured of her/his tenderness and care for the rest of our lives, if that is what we have promised? Are we willing to offer the same assurances in return?

In short, as we age, even when we are well, we are likely to be out of the bedroom more than we are in it. Let us be certain we really know a person before we consider any form of relationship, whether or not we want the relationship to include having sex.

If we do hope to enjoy sex, let's protect ourselves in every way. Remember that the prevalence of AIDS becomes *greater* as we age. But we should never get talked into doing something we don't want to do. Ever.

The best way I can close this chapter is to encourage you to listen to your heart.

We don't realize how important it is to have someone to remember with.

— *Silent Night, Lonely Night*
television film

Note: The same young granddaughter whose astute observations of my manuscript inspired this chapter wrote me an email just after completing her reading. "I am now contemplating writing a book titled *Dating for Teens,*" she revealed, and asked whether I had "any ideas." What came to my mind was her telling me last winter that "dating" meant "sitting together in the school lunch room." (I suspected hers was going to be a very short book.)

Then she asked if I would edit it for her (she has written several other "books," to her credit). She flattered me with, "You are the best editor I know, Grammie." She was of course setting me up. Naturally, I said yes.

She actually did write the book. It was five pages long. It needed no editing. And it was terrific.

BE THOU INSPIRED

What follow are some quotes that I have collected over the past 20 or so years. They always move and inspire me, and it is my pleasure to share them. Use them freely in dating communiques. But if they are too sappy for you, you have my permission to skip this chapter. I will never know!

It costs so much to be a full human being. One has to abandon, altogether, the search for security and reach out to the risk of living, with both arms . . . one has to embrace the world like a lover.

— Morris West
The Shoes of the Fisherman

To try to understand a person, you must understand what he/she is *not* saying . . . what she/he perhaps will never be able to say.

— John Powell, *Why Am I Afraid to Tell You Who I Am?*

It is the heart afraid of breaking, that never learns to dance. It is the dream afraid of waking, that never takes a chance.

— Amanda McBroom "The Rose"

We need the crazy courage to invade our own privacy.

— *The Portrait*, television film

I measure by highlights, not by years.

— Michael Dorris
A Yellow Raft in Blue Water

The fault, dear Brutus, is not is our stars,
but in ourselves, that we are underlings.

— William Shakespeare
Julius Caesar

Happiness is not external; it's not what
you get *from* life, it's what you *bring* to life.

— Wayne Dyer, *Real Magic—
Creating Miracles in Everyday Life*

The heart is a home that has room for
every person it loves.

— Enid Bagnold
The Chalk Garden

Trust your gut, because your gut has had less experience than your mind with self-doubt.

— Deepak Chopra, MD

Whether you think you can or think you can't—you're right.

— Henry Ford

It means more to me to be loved now than it used to.

— Louisa May Alcott
Little Women

We like someone because. We love someone although.

— Henri de Montherlant

Problems are messages.

— Shakti Gawain

You are where you are because you think what you think. If you don't like where you are, change your thinking.

— Unknown

I saw in him an extraordinary gift for hope. . . . a "romantic readiness."

— F. Scott Fitzgerald
The Great Gatsby

Busyness is no substitute for intimacy.

— Unknown

If life is to be enjoyed, then later isn't really an option.

— Julie Kurnitz

When nothing is sure, everything is possible.

— Margaret Drabble

Never, never, never quit.

— Winston Churchill

A DIFFERENT SORT
OF LOVE STORY

If love can happen as we age, then those of us who may have been resigned to giving up, at this point in our lives, are in luck.

This means that we are *not* crazy to think that dating is a viable option for us. It may, in fact, be our only option if we want to love again.

I'd like to share with you a piece of our family's history. It's a dating story. And it's a love story. It is a testimony to the fact that love and its ensuing relationship *can* happen at any age. And, in fact, it often does.

The story is in honor and in memory of my parents.

They seemed to come suddenly upon happiness . . . as if they had surprised a butterfly . . . in the winter woods.

— Edith Wharton, *Ethan Frome*

There is every reason to believe that my mother and my father enjoyed a solid and loving relationship during the more than 57 years that they were together. They hugged and kissed, raised three happy daughters, traveled all over the world in their sixties, entertained impressively, sang and joked together, shared in each other's joys and sorrows, and always supported and took care of one another.

The year before my father died of Alzheimer's, at 87, he lost his memory . . . except for recognizing my mother, Rosa, my two sisters, and me . . . and remembering every word and melody of any song that had ever been written about a ROSE. And when he could do nothing else, he could still sing every one of them.

During his illness, my mother developed significant colon cancer, assumed to be stage four. When the doctor told my sisters and me, we stood in the hospital's family area, hugging and crying hysterically for an hour. When he told my mother, she responded, "OK, so what are we going to do about it?" She was pragmatic and strong, but she had a poet's soul.

Her body was miraculous (she never, in her entire life, had a headache. She used to ask me what they felt like). She had her colon resectioned and a grapefruit-sized tumor removed. The doctor explained that when he received what turned out to be a stage one report, he thought a mistake had been made and that the report referred to another patient. Mother never even needed radiation or chemotherapy. The doctor claimed that the only possible explanation for the findings was that an angel had been sitting on her shoulder during her surgery.

Between my father's death and her ninetieth birthday (approximately three years), my mother continued to make short trips with us by car and plane. She also continued to entertain at home, to eat in fine restaurants (often administering her insulin shots, under the tablecloth overhang and through the fabric of her skirts), to watch college basketball games on television, to attend theatrical performances, to shine at parties (she was nicknamed "Pearl Mesta," Washington, DC's, most famous hostess of that era). She never missed an opportunity to flirt, effortlessly, with men much younger than I, wherever and whenever she met them.

At age 90, my mother suffered a major stroke. She lost most of her faculties. She couldn't speak, walk, feed herself, or recognize anyone. Sadly and reluctantly, we moved her to a nursing home. My sister and I visited her after work, at least every other day.

Some months passed, and her angel began visiting again. My mother began to recover. It was mystifying. When she reached the point at which she could go into the dining room for meals, first in a wheelchair and then walking, we would often join her for lunch. By this time, she was eating independently, conversing well, remembering most things, and being "Mom," meaning she noticed when we weren't wearing "enough" jewelry or hadn't styled our hair to her liking!

One day, when we joined her for lunch, she pointed out a well-dressed gentleman who was sitting at a nearby table. "That's [I'll call him] David," she announced. I have known him since I was in my twenties, before I met your Daddy. Go say hello to him," she ordered, in typical Mom fashion. Of course, we did.

Subsequently, we began to notice that whenever we came

to see her, Mom would be sitting on a settee with David, quietly reminiscing and discussing their families and, all the while, holding their heads quite close together. In time they would also be holding hands.

The staff and residents were abuzz. Apparently, David, an attorney of 95 who was still receiving office briefs for his approval, was courting my mother. She loved it. He walked her to her room at night, either kissing her at the door or sitting by her bedside until she fell asleep. They had become inseparable.

One warm day, I approached them as they sat outside on a bench, whispering. The infusion of youth was apparent in their faces when they asked me to take them for ice cream. I promised I would another day, knowing that I would not be allowed to take David, who was not a family member, off the premises. It still saddens me.

My mother, at 91, was in love again. And maybe what the two of them were sharing was not dating, in the conventional sense, but it was dating nonetheless.

At age 97, David traveled alone, by plane, to visit his family for the holidays. He had a wonderful trip. The following evening, he sat down on his bed, gently fell backwards onto his pillow, and died.

My mother was then 93. The nurses and aides feared she might suffer a dangerous reaction if she learned the news about David from a resident or stranger. They knew there would be consequences, in any case. So the entire staff that was on duty entered Mother's room, en masse, to inform her personally of David's death. They brought the obituary notice to her to help her understand, and they tried to soften her reality.

But their fears were realized. My mother's health spiraled downward after David's passing. And she never mentioned him again.

Yet, she continued to love her family's visits and our gentle conversations. David was replaced by stuffed animals that she cradled like babies. (She lamented that a woman could not have babies throughout life.)

Still having lucid moments at age 94, she began to "hear" my father singing. "Do you hear him?" she would ask, looking raptly at the ceiling. Her case worker from Hospice, who enjoyed the fleeting "spiritual" moments they sometimes shared, was convinced that "Rose is the luckiest of people . . . for she has one foot in this world and one foot in the next."

Mother continued to thrill to my father's singing until she died, three months before her 95th birthday.

There are no right answers. But there is a right question. It's the one that rubs up against our self-righteousness, resistance and fears. . . .

When you ask yourself, "Why not?" you may find yourself in motion, across a vivid and unpredictable landscape, over impossible mountains and beyond the water's edge, where you surprise yourself, once and for all, by getting wet.

— Karen Maezen Miller
Momma Zen

TO MY MUSES
WHO HELPED ME UNDERSTAND LOVE

To my father, Milton, who was the first man I ever loved and who was the first man ever to love me. To my mother, Rosa, who found the second love of her life at age 91. To my tender-hearted sister Gail and to my loving sister and brother-in-law Janet and Alan, who are my marital heroes. To my sons Adam, Peter, and Jason, who are the major part of my love story. To my glorious grandchildren Riley Rian, Olivia, Amanda, and Michael, step-grandchildren Jack and Ivan, and their lovely mothers Ilene, Kim, and Lisa, each of whom has deepened the quality of love in my life. To my relatives and friends, past and present, who have dated much or little, successfully or unsuccessfully, gotten married or not gotten married, stayed married or not stayed married, but who are living their lives with hope and enthusiasm. And to the pets of my life, each of whom could teach us all about unconditional love.

ABOUT THE AUTHOR

Sharon P. S. Marx (née Sharon Pearlman) was born and bred in Louisville, Kentucky, to which she has returned after having been well educated in Maryland and having enjoyed "a bunch of years" raising her three sons in the New York area. She would move again for the man who significantly stirs her heart. Sharon is 71 and admits that she is "anticipating with glee" the possibility of one more long-lasting romantic relationship. "It's in the genes!"

Always be in love, I remind myself, yes, definitely.

— Gloria Vanderbilt